A Triptych of Birds

and
A Few
Loose F e a t h e r s

PRATIBHA CASTLE

First published 2022 by The Hedgehog Poetry Press

Published in the UK by
The Hedgehog Poetry Press
5, Coppack House
Churchill Avenue
Clevedon
BS21 6QW

www.hedgehogpress.co.uk

ISBN: 978-1-913499-36-5

This book is dedicated with love and gratitude to my mother, Julia, who was also a lover of birds.

HEARTSEASE

They swoop in
a whimsy
of long-tailed tits.

Do they sense
from afar
spider hatchlings
swarming over terracotta pots
seed stash pansies
forsythia tipping yellow.

My heart hankering
for their cabrioles
of joy.

Contents

SOUTH DOWNS

Wolf sense idles me
into a random field
where sheep
take a brief break
from munching grass
to glance my way.

A black face dam fixes me
with Satan gaze,
transmits a cipher
I likely misconstrue, watches
as I mount the stile, swing
my leg across as if
the worn wood
is the saddle
of an imaginary mare
set to canter me off
into a fae mist distance.

Beyond the field
a path through the woods
petals open
into a copse,
incense of wild thyme, garlic,
blooming beneath my feet.
Blowsy clematis
tosses into a breeze
wafts the fantasy
of a cuckoo.

Dryads lean in,
anoint me with
murmured prayers.

I drift, in wonder
at a feather
amongst the leaves
from the red kite
keening in the blue, flash
above the brook of turquoise,
shadow splash of heron.

A CELTIC SPELL

He kept watch outside the back door
from a skeleton forsythia
choked past hope by an alpha jasmine.
Buffed his beak on a knuckley twig,
flounced his tail, bounced down
onto the terrace for a wary recce.

Gran told tales of Celtic lore, of a blackbird's luck,
how they augured weather, death.
In a clutch of days, he wheedled
a cranny in my heart. Mystic whistles
wooed me, swelled my chest
with an ache to shout out secrets.

When I hipped a basket to the carousel,
he flustered back into the bush.
I pegged out socks, a tea towel,
baby vest. His onyx eyes,
kohled with gold, reminded me
of you. Discovering

his taste for mealy worms, I bought
a tub, ripped off cardboard, bubble
wrap, prised open the lid, scattered
the desiccated corpses. The bird
scrutinised my every move, his tail flick
the black fan flirt of a señorita.

He fluttered to the worms, bobbed
his head from side to side as if
negotiating traffic, gobbled.
A sparrow came. The blackbird
chased him off. The sparrow's hen
risked a peck and scarpered. So did a wren.

He greets me now with a chuckle,
and a whirr of wings.
When I dribble out his feast,
he quivers on a flower pot,
trumpets a salute,
swoops in to dine.

The forsythia is showing shoots.
I miss the wren.

SPARROW LOVE

The female flirts her tail,
flamenco flounce
of a doyenne cute
at charm. Thumbs
up for the male, a coy

first timer, by the looks
of his several efforts
till the deed is done.
When she whisks
into the nest to sort,

I presume, the housekeeping,
he is quick to follow, now
he's got the hang of things,
no doubt eager to improve.
A flutter, till he arrows

from beneath the eaves
to return in a tail's flicker
to the drain. Where he struts,
the *bon mot* of a small white
feather in his beak, proof

to The Beloved how fine
a catch he is. As I dream
of its kiss against my
cheek, the cot this snowy boon
will fashion for its prize of eggs,

brown speckle glazed
with the suspicion of a sheen,
an image drowns my heart.
My father, his eyes behind
black rimmed glasses shiny

with incipient grief. Tears I caught
the hint of once, the day my mother
bundled me into a taxi, scrambled after.
Not a mention of it, ever, in the access hours

I idled with him at the flicks, over
milk shakes in the Wimpy Bar,
doughnuts, ice-cream cones. Apart
from that last day in St. Michael's hospital.
Two weeks and not a word.

His eyes opened. *Vron, I've missed you,*
an ocean streaming down his cheeks.

PADRAIG – WHO DROVE THE SNAKES OUT OF IRELAND

At the allotment, daddy
forked the crumbly black earth
till the air quaked
with anticipation of excess,
me sifting stones
in search of treasure;
the robin sat, pert,
on the lip of the bucket meant
to carry spuds or cabbages,
the occasional giggle-tickle carrot
back to placate the mammy.

The bird's eye bright
with a lust for worms,
his song a crystal cataract
of merry; though none
of the seeds we sowed
ever showed head
out of the sly earth
and we saw nothing
of the slow worm
daddy promised so that,
his name being Padraig too,
I guessed he must be a saint, especially
when he himself vanished.

Though he turned up
months later
at the end of school
again and again and again
till I had to tell the mammy
where the books and toys came from
and that got me sent off
to board at St. Bridget's convent
where the head nun was nice to you
if your mammy gave her fruit cake
in a tin, bottles of orange linctus sherry,
a crocheted shawl like frothy cobwebs,

none of which my mammy could afford,
Padraig having banished more than snakes.

RIDDLES

How could you let her
snatch me from you?

From your arm
about me as I chant
the cat sits on the mat.

From you mentoring
my muddles before school,
while I kick a leg of poxy pine,
perched on a chair uptipped in *I don't care.*

A living doll with lumpen plait,
my finger savaged
as a dog-gnawed bone.
An indigo Pict, stain lipped

from sucking at the Parker
fount of knowledge, nun instructed
to elicit loops and curlicues
in the mode of medieval monks.

From you explaining *where
is not the plural of was,* your blush
as I sing-song the purpose
of stamens in flowers, at which

she purses citrus lips, slams
the door with one of
those looks, flays all life
out of the breakfast dishes.

From you and her smiling at me
as I curl in bed, puzzling
why you never smile that way
at one another.

KOALA

I had one as a child.

Just a toy, still,
fashioned out of real fur,
you could make believe
you clutched a panting life,
feed eucalyptus leaves
into a pink-moist mouth.

Black nose, leather claws, eyes
glass, like the marbles daddy as a lad
clicked around granny's yard.
A game he would have taught me
on the kitchen slabs
had mammy not objected.

To crash my measly cache
of *Popeyes, cats eyes, beach balls*
with the payback
of a copper-sparkled *Lutz*.
Slate beneath a grown man's knees
penance for the later folly

of assuming he could
reach back, reconstitute
smoke blur memories
of the child my mammy
snatched from his embrace.

I had one as a girl.
Black nose, leather claws, eyes
glass, that never wept.

UNDER THE BRIDGE

A steel dragon
thunders past,
leaves a smoke trail
in the sky, plea
for the child
below the bridge
with little shield
save gloves,
pudding bowl
school hat, miraculous
blue medal of *The Lady*.

Blue, the colour
of the First Ray,
Virgin's veil, capes
of *The Daughters of Mary*.
Innocence. Eve before *The Fall*.
Flowers whose tongueless bells
chime spells to snare the senses.

The child abandoned
to a bellow of coal
and the beast's
mad gallop
down the rails,
her scream silenced
by the train whistle's shriek.

Drab mac
peeled back
exposes male fright
moon white slug slick
on the zipper
glint of prurient eyes.

Pimple cheeks
of a *sleveen* melting
in the shadows
to return in sleep
on the back
of the beast, dependable
as a train blast's shrill defeat.

No cape to warm her now
just ice spite
clanking chugging churning.

HOMEWORK

She flushes at the triumph
of a last full stop. About to serve the lunch,
her father skims the tale. His smile
crumples to a frown. Voice

icicle strict, he charges her
to rip the pages out, strike
through the paragraph
at the bottom of the page
under last week's homework,
Miss Clarke's *well thought out,*
good work, spangly gold star.

A tale of the bedroom
with the daisy papered walls
they made her swap with daddy
for the room adjoining ma's.
Jock's bark at the plop
on the mat of envelopes:
thick cream, brown,
tissue thin the blue
of her school summer frock;
stamps she rescued from the bin:
monkeys, exotic blossom, the once a snake.

Post her father tidies
by the silver toast rack
pinch waist coffee pot
ironed copy of *The Times,*
on the breakfast tray
he hustles
of a morning
up to stooped Judge Droop
retired, and wheezing
still abed.

Of evening primrose spires,
their yellow hands bowling
towards the sun, cowering shut
from cloud or blackbird evensong.

No hint of tentacles that in the night
writhe from out the cupboard, drawer,
beneath the bed to slink, in dreams
inside the blankets.

DROWNING

Waves suck in,
cast out, yank you
off your feet, pummel
empty of breath, thresh
you in the shingle.

Down, down.
Panic, choke.

Bubbling from your mouth,
a plea, heart pound shout
gobbled by the swell.
Brighton pier-posts
wobble, a watery
smear, crab
fluxes into sand,
other bathers a jungle
of blurry legs, blasted-
speaker mumbles, squeals.

Suffocating.

Breath wrung out
of you the way your
mother's tough love
wrung out the sheet she
scrubbed rinsed scoured till
her hands were scalded red with
washing soda, effort. Puddles
on the draining board, the floor;
faded pink and gold flamingos
on her apron soaked through
to the quill from all that
splish splash sluice

to erase a stain stubborn
as sin even coaxing and
crooning, the salt tears she
wept throughout parching her
to a whip of winter skirmished kelp,
did little to appease. And the blight
of that day lingered. A haunt
in her eyes you puzzled
over, like the blood on
what had seemed
a blameless sheet.

EXODUS

In the Confessional at school's end
the priest's face has the sheen
of the girl's Mary Quant
nude lipstick.

She fidgets on the hassock.
Incense thralls her, and a fantasy
of hands milking themselves
behind the grille.

Words hiss. *Tell me, my child,*
tongue-click over cracked lips,
flicker in the priest's groin:
exactly what did yous do with him?

Three times the question.
Three times her reply.
A Judas crow.
I slept with him.

She gabbles through the penance,
Hail Mary twenty times,
seethes down the nave,
through a sea of sleepy motes,
scents of lilies, unctuous echoes.

Candles in the Mary chapel
gutter, flare; Our Lady
tails her from under
lidded eyes. Mute. Cold stone.

The church door groans, clangs shut
as she steps out into the yard,
out of her flaunt of piety,
out of Mother Church.

A crow on a grave stone
ruffles its wings, cackles
applause. Breeze tousles her hair.
Baptism of apple blossom, absolution.

DOMESTIC GODS

the house is full of them
spider demons spinning
lace to throttle flies

wood lice sprites
snuck in from the garden
to struggle up the stairs

each step a MacGillycuddy Reek gained
to drop   a minute later   back
onto the hall floor   where

they bicycle impossible legs
in a hopeless bid
to set the world to rights

Nightmare bodies
rushing to and fro
faces in Daliesque collapse

sunflowers fleeing
Van Gogh vases with a single ear
crazed suns sizzling ice skies

snake flames flickering
from out the grate
a shepherdess

who flounces her skirt
follows the sheep
over the cliff edge mantle

sole relic amongst
the splintered porcelain
beside the grate   her smile

domestic gods   the world
is full of them   so why not
ditch the auld fella

with the beard
give a go to
apron angels

PLUMS

I put words in a paper bag,
hid them in my pocket.
Forgotten, squished like plums,
they leaked, chastised
the skirt of my Mary dress
with stains of shame.

I buried them beneath a bush.
Hopes, dreams.
Longed for hugs.

When, months later,
moving (as we always did)
away, my parents
hopeful for a better job,
me to yet another
chalk-cheeked
clique of nuns,
bully girls
in chilly dorms,
priest pontificating
from the pulpit,
words left suffocating
in the mole blind
dirt could offer
little comfort.

I gave myself
to arpeggios,
rallentandos, chords,
spilt tears onto callous keys,
Adulated birds and trees,
bluebells, inhaled melodies
and trills of hope.

A woman, I returned, exhumed words
meant for savouring on the tongue,
to be broadcast with blackbird songs
and never a need to hide.

HIPPY CHICK BLUES

We collide at a pumpkin stall
down Portobello Market. You
assess the silver blue lustre
of a Crown Prince, I
caress the green mottle
of Kabucha, its skin
craggy as an old crone's hopes
or rocky crevices about Olympus.

Yellow peel Turk's Turbans glower in a pile.

We twirl, we swirl
beneath a hunter moon
into a dew glazed gloam,
charmed by the keen
of a penny whistle,
banshee yowl
of a turf-fire fiddle.

Mammy cautions *don't you flaunt*
your heart upon your sleeve
so I sit till after midnight
stricken by her third degree
and first love's fluster, embroider
right across my tit, which you
and later I will feel, a plump
crimson pumper, brethren
to the thorn snarled muscle
of the plaster Christ enshrined
beside the sapphire Mary
on the parlour mantle.

You wild eyed Ulysses. The twang
of your finger-lickin' Gibson
plucks from me
a young girl's fancy
as the plight of your jeans,
frayed as nerves,
suggests a stitch-up.
I oblige with bird track tack
of rainbow hues infused
with moon-hex fantasies,

and a couch stitch pumpkin
to curse your knee.

AN GORTA MOR (THE GREAT HUNGER)

To the calls of owls,
she stitches a doll's dress
out of star sprigged cambric
bought for curtains
in the Camden flat
where she and a fatherless child
play house. Home, a place

she's never known
having grown up
in many mansions
ten in her first ten years
where daddy in a funeral suit
laid place mats, side plates,
buffed knives and forks, served
Mammy's roasts, apple tart
and cream *a good plain cook*
on genteel faded Delft: willow print
bridges spanning lotus streams, coolies
with pails on poles, backs bent, pyjama rags
grasping famine arms and legs.

Her parents thankful for a roof,
all found, basement kitchen,
haunted, windows barred.
Legacy in their bones,
potato crops,
black fleshed, a glut
of rot. Stinking. Turfed

out of crofts by blade-vowel
landlords with moot right
to pie-slice, dole out
the misty isle.

The doll's arms crucifix.
Invitation to a hug,
pasty no-eyes,
no-lips face.

THE ONLY ONE WHO LOVES YOU

Spurning words that echoed like a curse,
I stuffed a duffel bag with blister packs of pills,
Mary Quant minis, fantasies of girls
threading daisies in the muzzles of guns;
fled to the Big Smoke. In a bedsit

by Kensington Gardens, I massacred steak
with the mallet of hate, a year on, turned vegan;
pioneer in '68 of pity for pool-eyed cows,
sheep, slate stare plaice.
Feigned compassion.

Strove to prove to myself
that I was worthy of love.
Strutted the nights away
with flautists, a harpist
whose healer's hands
strummed my strings;
drummer, his silk tipped stroke
nimble on the snare; callous guitarists
plucking tunes from out of smoke drifts.

Chanted mantras with Ram Dass
in a basement in Notting Hill,
dossed in a Maida Vale squat;
candles, calor gas stove, the one tap
drip drip in the bog beside the back door.
Made out, off my head, with a sweetheart
leaf Philodendron, burnt joss sticks
to placate Kali's horde of swords,
sweeten the vibes, man,
stench of cat lit no-one
from the Highgate commune
I crashed in next, ever emptied;
spooned marmalade from a jar half-full,
recycled from a skip.

Almost believed myself deserving of love,
till come the morning, I forgot. My heart
tenderised with grief discovering
the night my mother died,
love is an ether you can choke or float in.

SWANS

A young wife
without a hearth,
she fled the hills,
sisters, suarach sun,
treasures entrusted
to the stewardship of mist,
contentious drizzle, grief
slouch clouds. And

though each week in the Finchley flat
that was never home, mocked
by the tisk of a gas flicker fire,
she sifted soda with a scrimp
of salt into ash fine flour,
coaxed in milk soured
with a fist of lemon
for want of buttermilk,
her nurse's hands
cosseting the dough
into a farl, blessing
with the sign of the cross
and a nod to Our Lady
on the mantel; slices
fried with rashers for the taste. And

come the Saint's day,
she clipped shamrock
to the collar of her coat,
mauve, a favour to her eyes,
each time she wet the pot, the curve
of its white spout was a heart stab
memory of swans   gliding   gracious
above the tarry Blackwater, a mere
stone's toss from the graveyard
outside of Kells. Her heart

keening for green hills
lost till I took her home,
too late for eyes never more
to tear up at the sight of mossy slopes
or the mizzle that kept watch
through grey days.

AFTERWARDS

After they took away the body,
the nice young men in green
uniforms, their eyes shiny,
like everyone's that day,
their voices the soothe
of pigeons' on the roof:
best not watch, love,
steep stairs, know what I mean?
Better off in the garden.

You shred a forget-me-not, recall
the hike up Benbulben Mount,
her eyes squinting as she explained
about her and Daddy.

After, once the ambulance
has left, at the *Crown*
and Shamrock, you
weep into a glass
of Merlot, large,
fidget the pearl rosary
you loosened from her fist.
The waitress (from County Clare,
her eyes the same quare blue
of Mammy's that,
according to the fancy
of the moon, flashed
crazy like a Kildare mare) nodding
as you hiccup how you'd
dropped by for tea
with a batch of scones
to find herself abed.
Asleep, you'd thought,
till you saw her fingertips,
a ruin of fallen plums.

The napkin sops, a Glencar
gush of tears, your
heart of ice you took
for hatred, melting; loosed,
like one of Grandda's racers,
only this was a race
already run.

WILD LASS OF KELLS

She shuffles on the kerb outside *O'Shaunessy's*, corner of Kelly and Dunleven Road. Her eyes the colour of Our Lady's veil, scorched bluer by her copper curls. On the lookout for the Da. Her task of a Friday night to wheedle the wages off of him before he sets out on the lash. Glad of a break from the chores. Socks like a flock of crows, forever jostling, hand me down frocks in need of hems, pants snagged on barbed wire, nails, atop of farmer's walls and fences. Herself, the firstborn of a baker's dozen; endless mopping up of spats, snail snots, scabby porridge pots.

Licks of laughter, yellow light, sidle out the gaping door into the night, let out by culchies on their shuffle to the bar. Eejits with purple slurs for eyes, glances tossed her way

collection plate
clink of small change at
Sunday mass

The odd time, a flash of lust; the most times, shame. A rare smile to build her up, *Sure aren't you a dote now, Delia, looking out for yer Mammy. God bless yourself.*

Eyes cast down, pious daughter of The Virgin, *Lord luv the child,* in her wilting dress, miraculous blue medal clipped to the chest of her tatty cardigan. An occasion of sin, *to be sure, sleveens might take advantage of.* Till she glances up. That glare, brazen as hell's fires, from the child of *Maire of the Scry Eye*, seventh daughter of a seventh son.

flame hex
of a
wild blood tinker

Skipping off home to a last scald of the pot, wedge of soda farl thick with dripping, her pocket is a clatter of coins, only the lighter by a bleary-eyed pint.

DAWN WALK

The sea sparkles,
a glimmer
of fallen
stars, glint
on the horizon
of coral light. I pause

at the water's edge,
bowl my hands
as if dawn
might be
cradled like
a gull's egg. Waves

sluice the shore,
the legs of an
oyster catcher
stood, head bent,
a prophet
hearkening;
my bare toes

scrabbling at lines
fine as capillaries.
Mysteries clammed
in sand and heart,
dissolving as I watch. Sun

seeping through the clouds
is an ache for my mother's smile
at our chance meeting
by The Cross when,
instead of spoiling her
with tea and craic,
I hurried on.

BELLS

tongue tales, drape chimes
amongst the village gables,
felted headstones, limbs
of the druid oak,
guardian of souls. Bells

joust the night air, bats
silking from under
chapel eaves, court
owls' sighs, dusk codes
sealed by day in mausoleum hearts.

Your voice is lost
to me and your sun blaze smile
when I dropped by
without a warning.
Your laughter

silvering the sky, a fete
of wedding bells
sobering to a sermon,
Thursday night bell drill
with its risk of a scorch

on careless hands. Rope
manhandled, a nudge
to let go lest it
hoist you up into
the chapel rafters.

Closer my God to Thee.

Your nurse's instinct
must have warned when you
spurned the doctor's counsel
and remained at home.

Does it always come too soon,
like a blackbird's
summons out of sleep?

ON REACHING HEAVEN

Your eyes the bubble sparkle
of a Moet sláinte,
you'll float across
in that cherry cardigan
you favoured towards the end.

Stuck at home, you
toasted the hours with
a click of needles knitting
socks for friends. I dropped by,
or phoned, less often than I later
wished though that last time I brought
the cake. A treat we'd baked together years
before; your strong hand on mine steering
the heart beat symmetry of the wooden
spoon through an anarchy of icing
sugar, butter, splash - or more,
dependant on the mood -
of Bewley's coffee.

The spill of your
song fizzing
the shadows
of the basement
kitchen as I jammed
together sponges open
hearted as your love.

The glory of walnut halves tallied
one to ten onto my palm
to be set with caution
on the buttercream
glaze. Baked
in honour
of the day,
the sun with its
celebratory gleam,
unseasonable. Tenth
of the tenth. The date
you and I each entered
this world and that you
even with your sixth
sense never guessed
would be the day
you'd leave.

REFUGE

I tend a wild garden

a bawdy house
of scent
and sound
and shade
where roses
toss their manes
in the style
of Connemara nags
marigolds scorch the soul
with orange zeal
nasturtiums writhe
with promiscuous
lithe ache about
the willow   where
a blackbird   sentinel
of whispered trysts
and the pond's gold wiles
trumpets a salute
to gypsy snails
emerald jewel beetles
tumble bees squiffy
on the damask malt
of antirrhinum
jasmine   thyme

sparrows in the bay bush
squabble   sputter
certainties and seeds

flurry of long tailed tits
woodpecker   bully of the fat ball
acrobatic finch

on a lounger
by the pond
Medbh on my knee
a furry shell
a tractor's grind
across the fields
becomes a purr

PIPE'S WAKE

Sifting the week before
through hair clips,
scarlet Alice band,
down-at-heel nail files
for the euphemism of a
scarf, it brushed your hand
the way the cat on every
visit nudged your shin.

Thin tin, red lip
fipple, mute
in lavender and silk
with *yer Uncle Mattie gone*
and though he never held a job,
he made that whistle sing.

The funeral morn, damp.
Timpani of droplets
on the window,
roof, your
marble heart.

At the grave, breeze
mussies your hair, keens
promises it will not keep.
You loose the pipe
from its silken shroud,
your sigh,
a kiss.

GLOSSARY OF IRISH WORDS

sleveen - untrustworthy or cunning person

suarach - paltry

craic - a good time

sláinte - good health, good time

ACKNOWLEDGEMENTS

My thanks to editors of the following publications in which these poems first appeared: *Bonnie's Crew, Blue Nib, Dreich, Eunoia, Fragmented Voices, HU, Impspired, Live Encounters Poetry & Writing, Lothlorien Poetry Journal, One Hand Clapping, Old Water Rat Publishing, Poetry and All That Jazz, Reach, Saraswati, Sentinel Literary Journal, Spilling Cocoa on Martin Amis, The Dawn Treader, Words for the Wild.*

Deep gratitude to all who have encouraged me to arrive at this point. Simon Jenner, who urged me on from the beginning; Naomi Foyle, for encouragement and mentoring; the wonderful tutors of what at the time was the English and Creative Writing Department, University of Chichester. Many poets and friends who have read and shared comments on these and other poems. All those who have listened to and appreciated these poems. Members of the Chichester Stanza. Poets in the Wednesday Poetry Retreat: Howard Timms, Marilyn Timms, Camilla Lambert, Clair Chilvers. Also Mandy Pannett, Chris Hardy, Raine Geoghegan. Other friends who have given help and suggestions for the cover; Jason Conway for his final design. A big thank you to Mark Davidson, editor of Hedgehog Poetry Press for awarding *A Triptych of Birds and A Few Loose Feathers* joint winner of Nicely Folded Paper Trois. And to my husband, a mathematician, for being open to discover the magic of words.